THE ILLUMINATED KADDISH

Interpretations of the Mourner's Prayer

THE ILLUMINATED KADDISH

INTERPRETATIONS OF THE MOURNER'S PRAYER

paintings, calligraphy and interpretations

by

Hyla Shifra Bolsta

KTAV PUBLISHING HOUSE, INC.

Library of Congress Cataloging-in-Publication Data Bolsta, Hyla.

The illuminated Kaddish: interpretations of the mourner's
prayer / Hyla Bolsta

p. cm.
Includes bibliographical references.
ISBN 978-1-60280-191-2

1. Kaddish. 2. Judaism--Liturgy--Texts. 3. Jewish illumination of books
and manuscripts. I. Kaddish. English and Aramaic. II. Title.
BM670.K3B65 2011
296.4'545--dc23

2011033483

KTAV Publishing House, Inc.,
888 Newark Avenue, Suite 119
Jersey City, N.J. 07306
Phone: 201-963-9524·Fax: 201-963-0102
Website: www.ktav.com
Email: orders@ktav.com

Dedicated to Laura Mitzner

MAY HER SWEETNESS MERGE WITH THE TREE OF LIFE

The Hand of Creation guides her from burgeoning earth, to sky and beyond.

CONTENTS

Mourner's Kaddish Transliteration and Hebrew (2)

L'ayla l'ayla min kol
birchata v'shirata tushb'chata
v'nechemata, da-amiron b'alma,
V'imru, AMEN.

Y'hay sh'lama rabba min sh'maya,
v'chayim alaynu v'al kol
Yisrael, V'imru, AMEN.
Oseh shalom bimromav,
hu ya'aseh shalom
alaynu v'al kol Yisrael,

V'imru, AMEN.

לְעֵלָּא לְעֵלָּא מִן כָּל
בִּרְכָתָא וְשִׁירָתָא תֻּשְׁבְּחָתָא
וְנֶחֱמָתָא, דַּאֲמִירָן בְּעָלְמָא,
וְאִמְרוּ, אָמֵן.

יְהֵא שְׁלָמָא רַבָּא מִן שְׁמַיָּא,
וְחַיִּים עָלֵינוּ וְעַל כָּל
יִשְׂרָאֵל, וְאִמְרוּ, אָמֵן.

עֹשֶׂה שָׁלוֹם בִּמְרוֹמָיו,
הוּא יַעֲשֶׂה שָׁלוֹם
עָלֵינוּ וְעַל כָּל יִשְׂרָאֵל,
וְאִמְרוּ, אָמֵן.

Mourner's Kaddish Transliteration and Hebrew (1)

Yitgadal v'yitkadash
sh'may rabba,
B'alma di v'ra chirutay,
v'yamlich malchutay
b'chayaychon uv'yomaychon
uv'chayay d'chol bayt Yisrael,
ba'agala u'vizman kariv,
V'imru, AMEN.

יִתְגַּדַּל וְיִתְקַדַּשׁ
שְׁמֵהּ רַבָּא,
בְּעָלְמָא דִּי־בְרָא כִרְעוּתֵהּ,
וְיַמְלִיךְ מַלְכוּתֵהּ
בְּחַיֵּיכוֹן וּבְיוֹמֵיכוֹן
וּבְחַיֵּי דְכָל־בֵּית יִשְׂרָאֵל,
בַּעֲגָלָא וּבִזְמַן קָרִיב,
וְאִמְרוּ, אָמֵן.

Y'hay sh'may rabba m'varach
l'alam ulalmay almaya.

יְהֵא שְׁמֵהּ רַבָּא מְבָרַךְ
לְעָלַם וּלְעָלְמֵי עָלְמַיָּא.

Yitbarach v'yishtabach v'yitpa-ar
v'yitromam v'yitnasay v'yithadar
v'yitaleh v'yithalal shmay
d'kudsha B'RICH HU,

יִתְבָּרַךְ וְיִשְׁתַּבַּח וְיִתְפָּאַר
וְיִתְרוֹמַם וְיִתְנַשֵּׂא וְיִתְהַדָּר
וְיִתְעַלֶּה וְיִתְהַלָּל שְׁמֵהּ
דְּקֻדְשָׁא בְּרִיךְ הוּא,

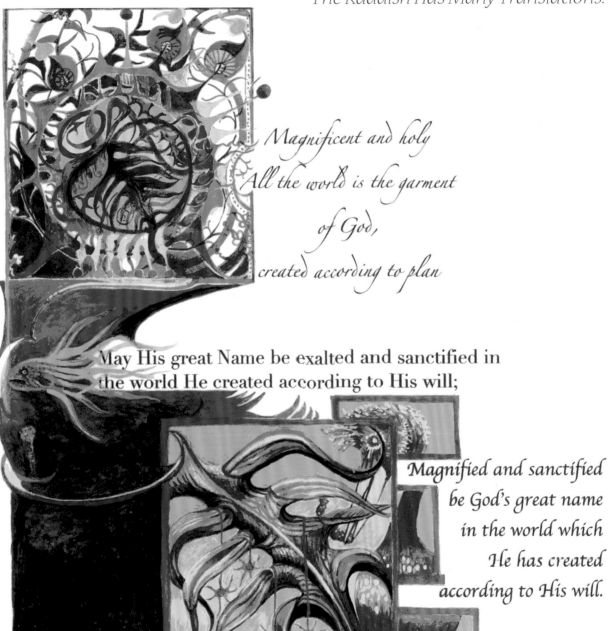

Magnificent and holy
All the world is the garment

of God,

created according to plan

May His great Name be exalted and sanctified in
the world He created according to His will;

Magnified and sanctified
be God's great name
in the world which
He has created
according to His will.

On the left are three examples of the first phrase.
Below is an interpretation of the prayer
by Rabbi Avram Davis.

Exalted and Sanctified is the Name of Loving Kindness
in this world,
Created According to the Intention,
And may it be established in Your Lifetime
and the Lifetime of the Community;
Speedily, Soon.   AMEN.

May this Name of the Infinite be blessed Forever;

Blessed and Praised, Glorified and Uplifted, Honored and
Elevated.
The Power of Chesed is Greater than all
the Hymns, Prayers or Consolations
We can Utter in this life.
AMEN.
May there be abundant Peace and a good life for all
The community;
For ourselves and for All Creation.
AMEN.
Mercy and Peace sustain the far heavens,
so may it Be for us,
For all the community, for all of Creation.
AMEN.

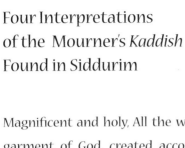

Four Interpretations of the Mourner's *Kaddish* Found in Siddurim

Magnificent and holy, All the world is a garment of God, created according to plan. In our lifetime we will see God's rule – soon it will come!

> And let us say, Amen.

The Great Compassion gives blessing – is blessing.

Glorious, exalted, honorable, extolled and elevated is this understanding.
The Great Compassion is greater than any words we might utter.

> And let us say, Amen.

May there be peace in all the world, for us and all who live,

> And let us say, Amen.

As there is peace in the supernal, may we be led to peace here, for us and all who live.

> And let us say, Amen.

May His great Name be exalted and sanctified in the world He created according to His will: And may He establish His Kingship during your lifetime and during your days and during the lifetime of the entire Family of Israel, Swiftly and soon.

> Now respond: Amen.

May His great Name be blessed forever and ever.

Blessed, lauded, glorified, extolled, upraised, honored, elevated and praised be the Name of the Holy One. Blessed be He Beyond all blessings, songs, praises and consolations that are uttered on earth.

> Now respond: Amen.

May there be abundant peace from heaven, and good life upon us and all Israel. He Who makes peace in His heights, may He make peace upon us and upon all Israel.

> Now respond: Amen.

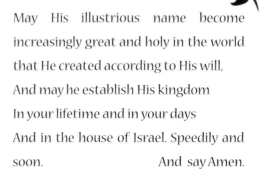

Magnified and sanctified be God's great name in the world which He has created according to His will. May He establish His kingdom soon, in our lifetime.

Let us say: Amen.

May His great name be praised to all eternity.

Hallowed and honored, extolled and exalted, adored and acclaimed be the name of the Holy One, though He is above all the praises, hymns, and songs of adoration which human beings can utter. Let us say: Amen.

May God grant abundant peace and life to us and to all Israel

Let us say: Amen.

May He who ordains harmony in the universe grant peace to us and to all Israel. Let us say: Amen.

May His illustrious name become increasingly great and holy in the world that He created according to His will, And may he establish His kingdom In your lifetime and in your days And in the house of Israel. Speedily and soon. And say Amen.

May His illustrious name be blessed always and forever.

Blessed, praised, glorified, exalted, extolled, honored, raised up and acclaimed be the name of the Holy one, blessed be He, beyond every blessing, hymn, praise and consolation that is uttered in the world.

And say Amen.

May abundant peace from heaven, and life be upon us and upon all Israel.

And say Amen.

May He who makes peace in his high places in his mercy make peace upon us and upon all Israel.

And say Amen.

PREFACE

I entered my studio one morning and paced, unable to concentrate, opened an art book on Breughel and turned to *The Triumph of Death.* A detail caught my attention. Death holds a violin and hovers over lovers making music. The image inspired me to paint two figures embracing, Laura and me. I knew her for forty-three years and I knew she was very ill. While I painted, these words came to me:

"As Death Lifted the Trumpet,
            They Embraced for the Last Time."

I finished in one sitting and walked to the house. Laura's brother called and told me that Laura had passed away. Her life ended as I laid down my brush.

As Death Lifted the Trumpet
They embraced for the last time

As Death Lifted the Trumpet They Embraced for the Last Time.

We embrace at the edge of our world. Death lurks behind me. Laura's face points towards Death but she nestles in my shoulder. The line of infinity gives us inspiration and breath. It will weave through the images and remind us that our lives are naught but Time and Space, set into infinite forms.

In the following months, I felt my friend's presence as I worked; Laura became my Muse. The first paintings were expressions of love and appreciation for her and my feelings about her death. I recited the Mourner's *Kaddish* by myself and in synagogue, and felt called to study it. Phrases flowed over and through me, painting after painting. Loss washed me in surges, especially when I worked on the last lines, when I believed the series was at its end and my Muse, my friend, would leave.

After painting twenty images, I asked Rabbi Margaret Holub, spiritual leader of the Mendocino Coast Jewish Community, to help me understand the Aramaic, word by word. We riffed on the phrases and discovered deep meanings and intimations. As we explored, I was transformed and found the prayer's magic. Reminiscent of Alice's story, it has been its own Wonderland.

16

SHE RISES ON A WING OF INFINITE LOVING KINDNESS

Fearless and relaxed, she lies on a magic carpet and plays with the clouds while threads of infinity draw her to themselves.

The delightful study stimulated me to create illuminated calligraphy of the text in Aramaic/ Hebrew and English. These texts correspond to the painted images yet stand alone as pages upon which to meditate, like medieval manuscripts.

Some pages have only one Hebrew/Aramaic word, with an English translation. In the *Kaddish*, verbs carry specific meanings hidden to most of us who don't know the language. Words of praise are balanced in such a way as to be like our ribs, holding our organs of life. No mention of death or God (only "The Great Name"), this is a prayer that brings the realm of the holy into the here and now. I have wandered in this prayer and it has opened me to its grandeur.

AS WE PASSED, FLOATING, FLYING, HER EXQUISITE NATURE WAS REVEALED.

Black-robed figures stand solid on earth's surface, clutching strings of attachment. Images of deceased spirits lift off, monuments to life. They are not far off or out of view.

INTRODUCTION

When family or friends pass away, loss runs rampant over us and dictates its needs; we discover who we are inside this new force. Jews begin the journey with the *Kaddish*, a prayer of sanctification, a doxology or text of praise. The custom began in the Middle Ages, but its gist reaches back to the Talmud.

Rabbis advise us to prepare for worship with meditation, songs and blessings. Such celebration readies the congregation for the Torah Service. We assemble, open to The Great Name and infuse our spirits with joy. How do we do this while grieving?

20

When we recite The Mourner's *Kaddish*, we join the vast ensemble of generations who invoked these same words in their times of sorrow. Countless millions of Jews have formed these phrases of exaltation while their hearts beat the rhythm of grief. They looked to heaven and asked why, sobbed, hunched in silence, tore their clothes, whispered bargains or accepted the will of God. Guilt-ridden or relieved, in one way or another, they mourned. In every synagogue the world over, weekdays and Sabbaths, mourners stand and daven with their peers and the congregation responds. The community shares the sensibility of life and death.

Tributes to any god could easily sound empty at a time of deep mourning when creative urges lie dormant and life's possibilities seem remote. But the custom encourages and nourishes a potential for lifted spirits and the prospect that these words open the soul to a different reality. And for some, the promise that when such phrases are uttered aloud, souls flutter, wings open and the heart begins a flight toward healing, for the living and for the deceased.

The Rabbis who gave us this devotion and the tradition of performing it knew what heals our hearts and the heart of this world. Repetition's familiar cadence transforms us. Rhythmic sounds help sooth and offer solace just as the same lullaby night after night reassures a baby to sleep.

A mourner chants the *Kaddish* and during those moments, time rests in praise.

With stanzas of gratitude, we enter sacred space and holy time, distinct from the mundane and separate from the rest of our lives.

In his prologue to *The Sabbath*, Abraham Joshua Heschel wrote, "Judaism is a religion of time aiming at the sanctification of time … there are no two hours alike. Every hour is unique and the only one given at the moment, exclusive and endlessly precious."

Our incantations voice reverence for life. We step into a world without mention of death or God (in the Aramaic; however, English translations use the word God). Lament, anguish, suffering, personal entreaty do not find purchase, only the intent to bring the whole world into *devukut* with The Name). (*Devukut* means an absolute love, melding into the Whole, like a garment woven without a seam or drops of water in a pool.)

22

We function in a world of routine, familiarity, yin and yang, separation, real or imagined. When we pray, we give ourselves an opportunity to leave all this behind and create new imprints in our cells, minds and all our organs.

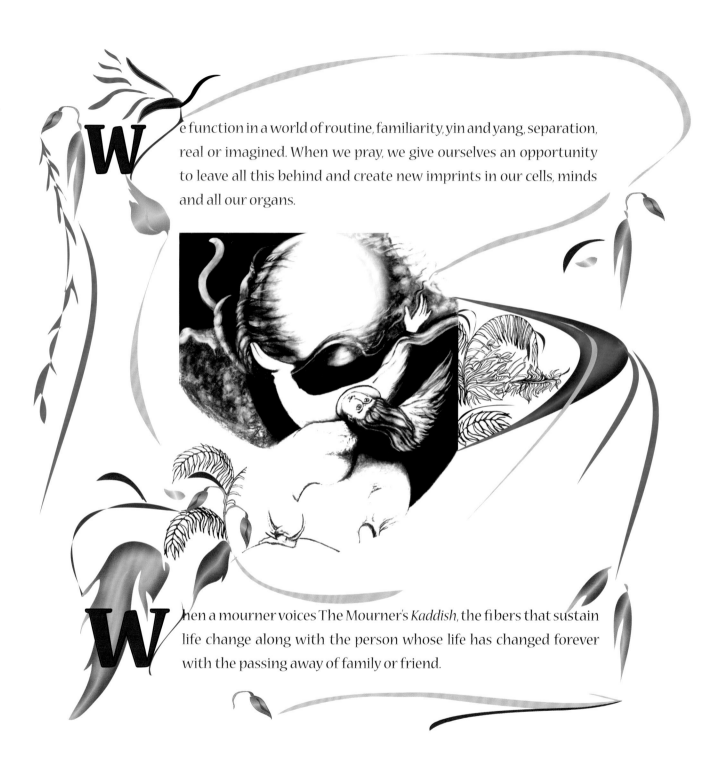

When a mourner voices The Mourner's *Kaddish*, the fibers that sustain life change along with the person whose life has changed forever with the passing away of family or friend.

PART I

CALLIGRAPHIC

ILLUMINATIONS

יתקדש שמה רבא

May the Great Name Grow in holiness

shower us with its evidence in wonder and sanctity, surround us
as we call out, be with us as we pray.

Yitgadal v'Yitkadash Sh'may Rabba

יתגדל ויתקדש שמה רבא

26

DERASH

YITGADAL V'YITKADASH SH'MAY RABBA:

MAY THE GREAT NAME GROW

AND BE SANCTIFIED

From our first moments of
mourning we appeal that
Creation's Spirit enlarge
and be holy, responding to
the smallness we feel and to
HaShem's diminished world, now
that one life is lost
to creation.

A SOURCE WITHIN ITSELF

THE GREATNAME SHALL EXPAND THROUGH OUR PRAYER

IT grows Itself

יתגדל

our prayer for death begins with growth and holiness

from the smallest letter to the largest

the WORD ITSELF is growing

REFLEXIVE INTONATION COMMAND FUTURE

AN ACTIVE VERB

MAY IT GROW

Yitgadal

יתגדל

28

DERASH

YITGADAL: MAGNIFY YOURSELF

The first word presents Creation's
duality - growth in the midst of
death, expansion and contraction.
The Aramaic words are reflexive
verbs and refer back to themselves,
source themselves, act upon
themselves, and thereby carry
power. The same can be said of us.
As we embody life we
intertwine with
the growth of
The Great Name.
YITGADAL holds a key to the meaning of life,
the Self expands through Itself:
"I am that I am."

Set apart — HOLY

THE GREAT NAME
is special —
It is like no other

WE SET APART THIS NAME
AS WE SET APART
THE MOURNING TIME
IT IS LIKE NO OTHER

יתקדש

IT sanctifies itself

Yitkadash

יתקדש

30

DERASH

YITKADASH: SANCTIFY YOURSELF

The Aramaic implies both present and future. The prayer's first words command and hope that the presence of The Great Name is and will be manifest, as and because we call out. Through our plea, we imbue the atmosphere with the vibrations of these words. *HaShem's* essence grows in our consciousness and becomes more evident in this world.

His Great Name
שמה רבא

Already great, and now, with
us uttering this first line...
it grows in our consciousness

More evident in our atmosphere.
Accessible in this, our World.

The Divine Name Itself is
sanctified when we proclaim
faith in Its holiness in open prayer.

We call to the Great
Name – grow in our midst!

Sh'may Rabba

שמה רבא

Derash

SH'MAY RABBA: THE GREAT NAME

The opening words,

YITGADAL V'YITKADASH,

were inspired by

Ezekiel 38:23.

The prophet envisions a time

when God will become great in

the eyes of all the nations.

בעלמא די ברא כרעותה

B'alma di v'ra chirutay

Derash

B'ALMA: IN THE WORLD

The Aramaic word, ALMA relates to the Hebrew OLAM, translated as "world." Here it signifies all dimensions and layers of worlds beyond worlds.

בחייכון מלכותה ימליך

וביומיכון

AND THE Majestic One Will Reign

This World will be imbued — with The Prescence

IN YOUR LIFE AND YOUR DAYS

Let the Great Name be Known... May earth be THE REALM... Be present among us..... May It fill your moments of life...

וימליך מלכותה .בייכן ובימכון

V'yamlich malchutay b'chayaychon uv'yomaychon

DERASH

V'YAMLICH MALCHUTAY:

THE MAJESTIC ONE WILL REIGN

A kingdom such as this
implies a huge scope,
beyond anything that
anyone could comprehend.
In Aramaic, words have
suffixes that change the
root form of the word
to abstractions and give
phrases broad meaning.

וּבְחַיֵּי דְכָל
בֵּית יִשְׂרָאֵל
בַּעֲגָלָא
וּבִזְמַן קָרִיב
וְאִמְרוּ
אָמֵן

AND IN THE LIFE
IN ALL THE HOUSE
OF ISRAEL
OF ALL THE GOD-WRESTLERS
OF ALL HERE NOW

MAY IT COME AROUND SOON
MAY IT BE CLOSE IN TIME
IN THE RUSH & ROLL OF TIME
A CIRCLE OF WHOLENESS
COMPLETING OUR LIVES

uv' chayay d'chol bayt Yisrael, ba'agala uvizman kariv. V'imru Amen.

וחיי דכל בית ישראל בעגלא ובזמן קריב. ואמרו אמן

DERASH

BA'AGALA UVIZMAN KARIV:

SPEEDILY, SOON, AMEN

The Aramaic word for "speedily" or "swiftly" stems from the same root as wagon, wheel, to roll, to be round and circle. Following this are the Aramaic words "time close" which we translate as "soon." The prayer embraces my imagination: "May the time of The Great Name's reign roll closer to us, moving like a chariot imbued with God," and I think of Ezekiel.

יהא שמה רבא מברך

MAY The Great Name Be BLESSED
FOR EVER AND EVER
FOR ETERNITY
AND ETERNITY
OF ETERNITIES
ALL TIME
ALL SPACE
AND IN ALL WORLDS
AND WORLDS BEYOND WORLDS

ולעלמי עלמיא

Y'hay sh'may rabba m'varach l'alam ulalmay almaya

יהא שמה רבא מברך לעלם ולעלמי עלמיא

DERASH

Y'HAY SH'MAY RABBA M'VARACH L'ALAM ULALMAY ALMAYA: MAY THE GREAT NAME BE BLESSED FOREVER AND EVER

The congregation joins the mourners. Why for this line, not others? Perhaps it is the rhythm and timing; at this point it is good to support the mourners and energize everyone.

Sages believe the significance is ancient and deep, stemming from Jacob's response on his deathbed, to his youngest son, Benjamin. Jacob lamented that his children would not keep the faith of Abraham and Isaac and this moved Benjamin to reply, "Hear O Israel *HaShem* is God *HaShem* is One." ("Israel" was Jacob's God-given name.) With this reassurance, Jacob replied, "Baruch shem kavod malchuto l'olam va-ed." "Blessed be His kingdom forever and ever."

The response is a public declaration of the belief that God is great and holy: Y'HAY SH'MAY RABBA M'VARACH L'ALAM ULALMAY ALMAYA (May His Great Name be blessed forever and ever). This is to be said with all the mental focus possible. A mystical interpretation is, "The Infinite Light should come into existence in this world, break through, channel into our three worlds of Creation (thought), Formation (speech) and Action (concrete reality). This response is central to the *Kaddish* and should be said out loud. Almost word for word, this phrase appears in the Book of Daniel 2:20. Similar phrases are also found in other parts of the Bible.

According to the Talmud, recitation of Y'HAY SH'MAY RABBA has potent cosmic effect and is the most essential part of the entire prayer.

יתברך וישתבח ויתפאר ויתרומם ויתנשא ויתהדר ויתעלה ויתהלל

שמה דקודשא בריך הוא

BLESSED AND PRAISED AND
UPLIFTED AND EMBELLISHED
BE THE NAME OF THE HOLY ONE

BEAUTIFIED AND ENLARGED AND
AND RAISED UP AND ACCLAIMED
BLESSED BE IT

This structure is like our symmetrical ribs, strong
and protective, housing and guarding vital organs.

Uttering four concepts = Blessed, Enlarged, Raised and Uplifted
invoking each two times, we wrap them around our thoughts
and we thus sustain our spirits.

Yitbarach v'yishtabach v'yitpa-ar v'yitromam v'yitnasay v'yithadar v'yitaleh v'yithalal

יתברך וישתבה ויתפאר ויתרמם ויתנשא ויתהדר ויתעלה ויתהלל

shmay d'kudsha b'rich hu   שמה דקדשא בריך הוא

DERASH

Hidden within The *Kaddish* lies an armature, a sturdy spine of sacred experiences, two sets of five complementary spiritual attitudes. They hold a symmetrical inner space, two sides of a ladder leading to the heavenly realms.

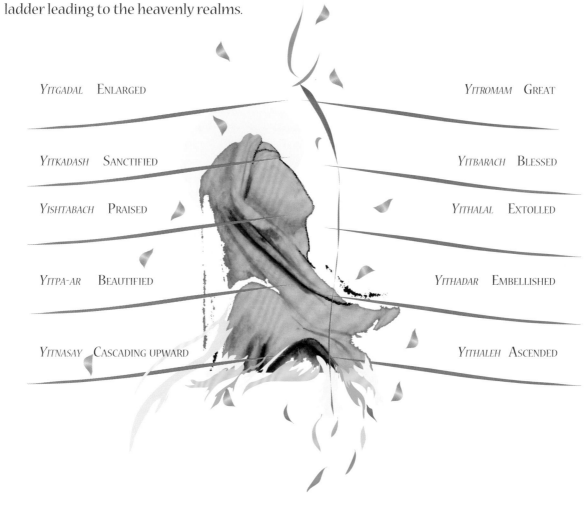

YITGADAL	ENLARGED	*YITROMAM*	GREAT
YITKADASH	SANCTIFIED	*YITBARACH*	BLESSED
YISHTABACH	PRAISED	*YITHALAL*	EXTOLLED
YITPA-AR	BEAUTIFIED	*YITHADAR*	EMBELLISHED
YITNASAY	CASCADING UPWARD	*YITHALEH*	ASCENDED

Above All
Greater than
BEYOND

OUR BLESSING
OUR SONG

OUR PRAISE
OUR COMFORT

לְעֵלָּא מִן כָּל
בִּרְכָתָא וְשִׁירָתָא

תֻּשְׁבְּחָתָא
וְנֶחֱמָתָא

דַּאֲמִירָן בְּעָלְמָא
וְאִמְרוּ אָמֵן

Which are said-uttered on earth ~ in all the dimensions-allworlds-time-space
And SAY AMEN

L'ayla l'ayla min kol birchata v'shirata tushb'chata v'nechemata da-amiron b'alma.

לְעֵלָּא לְעֵלָּא מִן כָּל בִּרְכָתָא וְשִׁירָתָא. תֻּשְׁבְּחָתָא וְנֶחֱמָתָא. דַּאֲמִירָן בְּעָלְמָא.

V'imru Amen.

וְאִמְרוּ אָמֵן

44

DERASH

L'AYLA L'AYLA MIN KOL BIRCHATA:

Can we imagine that above all we know, greater than any blessing we give, reciting the *Kaddish* for a loved one is greater than anything else we can do? How we perform this mitzvah, recite this prayer for our dead, is significant not only to ourselves but for all the world. According to tradition, when we recite this prayer, we help the world of the living and the world of those who have passed away. We do not know all its ramifications.

And Let There Be
GREAT PEACE
from HEAVEN AND LIFE
UPON ALL ISRAEL AND ALL
WHO DWELL ON EARTH AND SAY AMEN

שלמא רבא מן שמיא
וחיים עלינו ועל כל ישראל
ועל כל יושבי תבל
ואמרו אמן

May the one who makes PEACE
in the high realms make PEACE
Upon us and upon all Israel and
Upon all who dwell on earth AND SAY AMEN

עושה שלום במרומיב הוא יעשה
שלום עלינו ועל כל ישראל
ועל כל יושבי תבל
ואמרו אמן

Y'hay sh'lama rabba min sh'maya v'chayim alaynu — יהא שלמא רבא מן שמיא וחיים עלינו

v'al kol Yisrael v'al kol yoshvay tayval. V'imru amen. — ועל כל ישראל ועל כל יושבי תבל ואמרו אמן.

Oseh shalom bimromav hu ya'aseh shalom alaynu — עושה שלום במרומיב הוא יעשה שלום עלינו

v'al kol Yisrael v'al kol yoshvay tayval. V'imru amen. — ועל כל ישראל ועל כל יושבי תבל ואמרו אמן.

DERASH

Y'HAY SH'LAMA: LET THERE BE PEACE

Peace from within fosters the
possibility of greater access to an
open mind and heart and enhanced
understanding. And likewise, from
open mind, heart and understanding
comes peace. We pray for the world
by reciting this prayer.
We pray for all creatures,
for all sentient and non-sentient
beings, the trees, the rocks,
the salty oceans, all waters
and elements and all peoples
and animals dwelling on this plane.
For all who share this world
together:
May we find the way to Truth and
may we find the blessing of Peace.

page 26   **YITGADAL V'YITKADASH SH'MAY RABBA**

The words: May The Great Name grow in holiness, shower us with its evidence, in wonder and sanctity, surround us as we call out, bewitch us as we pray.

The illumination: Flames of Creation crown the words. Arms open, birds, fish, plants all move towards them.

page 28   **YITGADAL**

The words: It grows Itself. Our prayer when we face death begins with growth and holiness, from the smallest letter to the largest word Itself - is growing. A source within Itself, The Great Name shall expand through our prayer.

The illumination: Earth feeds and life grows. Mothers, fathers, offspring, flesh, sap, words, sounds, out to the atmosphere, back to the ground, all and everywhere; organic flow.

page 30   **YITKADASH**

The words: Set apart, holy, The Great Name is special. It is like no other. We set apart The Name as we set apart the mourning time. It is like no other.

The illumination: Birds, winged beasts, sea waves and plants symbolize holiness of Creation in each corner of the page and the world.

page 32   **SH'MAY RABBA**

The words: Already great, and now, with us uttering the first line, it grows in our consciousness. More evident in our atmosphere, accessible in this, our world. The Divine Name itself is sanctified when we proclaim faith in Its holiness in open prayer. We call to The Great name - Grow in our midst!

The illumination: The Tree of Life with ten *sefirot* nests in a pyramid of purity. The bird of life lifts all and carries the olive branch. All of life, the seas, plants, rocks and breathing beings rejoice in the threads of infinity.

B'ALMA

The words: In the world which was created as Her desire, in which The Great Name was pleased to and wanted to create, to delight in.

The illumination: Spiraling life, in its patterned intricacy, teems with creation, every part in movement, gracing every page of life.

V'YAMLICH MALCHUTAY

The words: And the Majestic One will reign. This world will be imbued with The Presence in your life and your days. Let The Great Name be known … be present among us … May earth be The Realm.
May it fill your moments of life - all.

The illumination: The Ruler sits on the throne of creation, animals play, flowers blossom in beauty and The Presence is a faceted jewel.

BA'AGALA

The words: And in the life in all the house of Israel, of all the God-Wrestlers, of all here and now - May it come around soon. May it be close in time in the rush and roll of time, a circle of wholeness completing our lives.

The illumination: The Queen rushes forward on Her Steed, wielding a ray of infinity. The mighty horse rolls the great wheels to the right; the dove flies to the left on her chariot of clouds and fire.

Y'HAY SH'MAY

The words: May The Great Name be blessed forever and ever, for eternity and eternity of eternities, all time, all space and in all worlds and worlds beyond worlds.

The illumination: The Tree of Life twists upward, sustains flesh and flower, water and air for infinity, and all the while The Bird-Shechina spreads Her wings, gives favor and protection to The Tree with a tender sprig.

YITBARACH V'YISHTABACH

The words: Blessed and praised and beautiful and enlarged and uplifted and embellished and raised up and acclaimed be the name of The Holy One. Blessed be The One. This structure is like our symmetrical ribs, strong and protective, housing and guarding vital organs. Uttering four concepts - Blessed, Enlarged, Praised and Uplifted - invoking each two times, we wrap them around our thoughts and we thus sustain our spirits.

The illumination: Winged lions balance in exaltation on the tree of life, whose roots become our world.

L'AYLA L'AYLA MIN KOL

The words: Above all, greater than, beyond - our blessing, our song, our praise, our comfort, which are said - uttered on earth - in all the dimensions - all worlds - time - space. And say, Amen.

The illumination: Throughout the infinite burgeoning of life, we reach towards the heavens, pray, wrap threads of fecundity into the endless eggs of the world and The Nameless One sparks life.

Y'HAY SH'LAMA RABBA

The words: And let there be great peace from heaven and life upon all Israel and all who dwell on earth. And say, Amen. May The One who makes peace in the high realms make peace upon us and upon all Israel and upon all who dwell on earth. And say, Amen.
Some congregations, i.e., Reconstructionist and Renewal, add the words in light grey.

The illumination: Inside the right wing of the soaring bird, the lion rests with the lamb, sheltered under the leaf of budding hope. God releases the dove that carries the olive branch and sheds rays from the night sky.
"What will be" rests on those hands and darkness moves through dawn into day.

The *Kaddish* alludes to our partnership with The Great Name.

We aid each other to become illustrious in this world.

We create and complete each other; we unite with The Divine.

PART II

PAINTINGS

VISUAL

INTERPRETATIONS

Magnificent

& holy   All the world is the garment of God

Kaddish for Laura

MAGNIFICENT AND HOLY ALL THE WORLD IS THE GARMENT OF GOD

Mother Earth, garbed in natural beauty, sources all we see; trees reach from dirt to sky, gracing flesh and spirit. They are, like us, like all, enduring, and ephemeral. The *New Oxford American Dictionary* states that a second meaning of "garb" is a sheaf of wheat. Indeed! The earth's clothes are vestments used to apparel God.

Exalted and Sanctified Is The Great Name

Spirit rises, gives blessing to dancers on top of the world.
Lamb and lion, woman and man, whirl to the music of peace
wrapped in lines of infinite joy.

Created ACCORDING to PLAN

CREATED ACCORDING TO PLAN

A breath of Creation cascades over the universe.
Woman and man spring from Her winged shoulders.
The departed passes through, carrying the infinite thread.

AND MAJESTY WILL REIGN IN THIS KINGDOM IN YOUR LIFE

The Shechina graces this world with Her touch. Trees of life originate in every direction. Crowns of leaves blossom and shelter all spirits in infinite threads.

IN OUR LIFETIME WE WILL SEE GOD'S RULE SOON IT WILL COME!
AND LET US SAY AMEN

The spirit of The Nameless One envelops the world. Carried in great strides, dark and light, we travel through infinity's ribbons of peace.

AMEN, MAY THE NAME OF THE GREAT TEACHER TRIUMPH.

Flaming hands reach towards the one who flies past three worlds, beyond the gates of time.
Hills of rivers ascend to the blossoming sun. Amen takes the departed into its light (and beyond).

May the Great Name be EXALTED and Sanctified
May This Name ~ Chesed ~ Lovingkindness
be blessed forever and ever. Amen

MAY THE GREAT NAME BE EXALTED AND SANCTIFIED.
MAY THIS NAME ~ CHESED ~ LOVING KINDNESS BE BLESSED FOREVER AND
EVER. AMEN.

We stand at the top of the world. Winds strew infinite threads of love, sparking flames of spirit.
We are bound with our dead as we exalt life.

The Great Compassion gives blessing
is blessing

THE GREAT COMPASSION GIVES BLESSING – IS BLESSING.

The Four hands of the four worlds of God descend in blessing.
We spread our arms and receive
the gift of life, dancers receiving the pulse of God's music.

BLESSED AND LAUDED AND GLORIFIED AND EXALTED AND UPLIFTED AND HONORED AND ELEVATED AND PRAISED.

We touch The Blessed and join our deceased in infinity. Praise wraps the hills and vales of
our days and prayer and strength grow the grass.

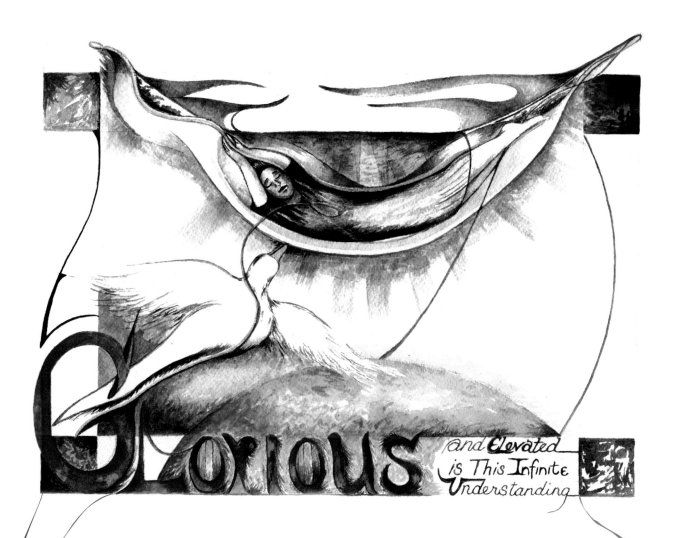

GLORIOUS AND ELEVATED IS THIS INFINITE UNDERSTANDING

She parts, rests softly in the hammock of the Dove of Peace, who gently guides her above the world.

THE GREAT COMPASSION IS GREATER THAN ANY WORDS WE MAY UTTER.
AND LET US SAY AMEN.

Compassion holds the departed and floods light to those in mourning.

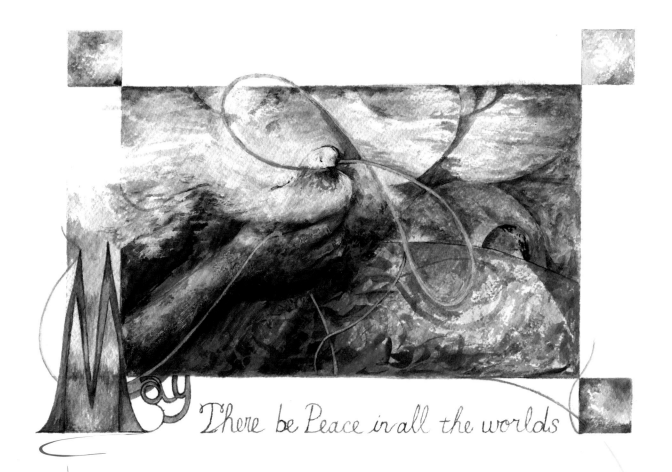

May There be Peace in all the worlds

MAY THERE BE PEACE IN ALL THE WORLDS

Feathers emanate from the Dove of Infinite Peace, held aloft by the Shechina.
They float through the heavens of the four worlds.

(The four worlds refers to the mystical teachings of the Kabbalah, that the universe is comprised of four worlds or levels of reality.)

*PEACE FOR US AND ALL WHO LIVE
AND LET US SAY AMEN.*

The Shechina envelops all creation, is all creation, and holds in her realm the threads of peace.

66

As there is Peace in the Supernal
May we have Peace in All the World.

As There Is Peace in the Supernal
May We Have Peace in All the World.

Hands of The Nameless One embrace, peace wraps itself gently
and the departed reaches to us, to give us peace.
"His left hand is under my head, and his right hand embraces me."
Song of Solomon, chapter 2 verse 6

AND LET US SAY AMEN.

Flaming hearts, through shadow and mist, say good-bye, let go the strings, and all say Amen.

As Amen Is Sung with All Our Strength the Sacred in All Shines Everywhere.

Lit by the flames of sacred passion, each soul carries its world, lifts its face to the heavens where
The Nameless One forms the fire of life and blesses the worlds with feathered hands.

PART III

QUOTES

FROM

RABBIS

SCHOLARS

AND

TORAH

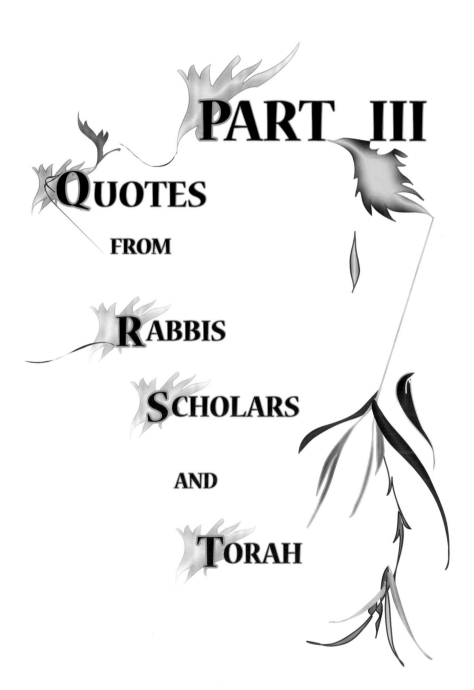

One prays for peace

more than for any other blessing.

You might say -

"Here is food and drink," but if there is no peace, there is nothing.

Hence, "I will give peace in the land" (Leviticus 26:6),

suggesting that peace outweighs everything else.

Likewise it is said (Isaiah 45:7):

"I make peace and create everything."

Paraphrase of an excerpt from Judah Ben Yakar's

Interpretation of the Liturgy (c.1200–1205)

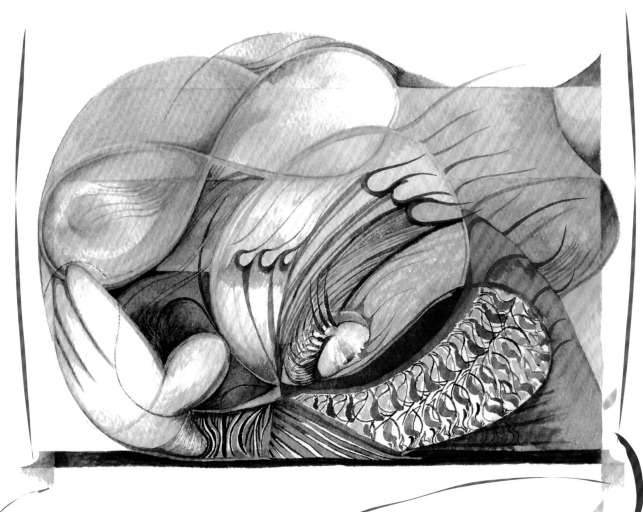

THIS ONE TOOK SOLACE IN PRAYER

Immersed in prayer, worlds upon worlds protect her; the mundane mind shrinks; her open hand grows and opens to grace.

Prayer

of Reb Nachman of Bratslav

Master of the Universe,

grant me the ability to be alone;

may it be my custom

to go outdoors each day

among the trees and grass,

among all growing things

and there may I be alone,

and enter into prayer,

to talk with the One to whom I belong.

May I express there everything in my heart,

and may all the foliage and the field -

all grasses, trees and plants -

awake at my coming,

to send the powers of their life

into the words of my prayer

so that my prayer and speech

are made whole

through the life and spirit

of all growing things,

which are made as one by their

transcendent Source.

May I then pour out words of my heart

before your Presence like water, O Lord,

and lift up my hands to You in worship,

on my behalf, and that of my children.

adapted from R'Natan, *Likutey*

T'filot, l:52, ll:11, ll:22

75

Judaism perceives life

and all the dimensions of life, as cycles. Everywhere we look, there are cycles . . . cycles of birth and dying, sickness and health. Our life is one cycle. That is, we are only here for the weekend.

Rabbi Avram Davis, *Arising of Wisdom Heart*

You think

that you pray to God.

Prayer IS God!

Rabbi Pinchas of Koretz

(1728–1790) *The Imrei Pinchas*

When wood burns

it is the smoke alone that rises upwards, leaving the grosser elements below.

So it is with prayer. The intention (*kavanah*) alone ascends to heaven.

Ba'al Shem Tov

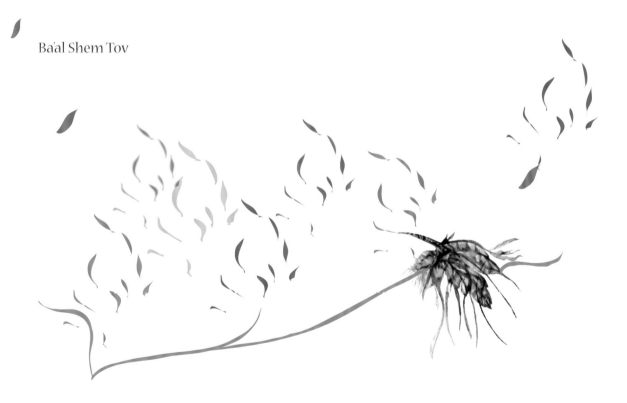

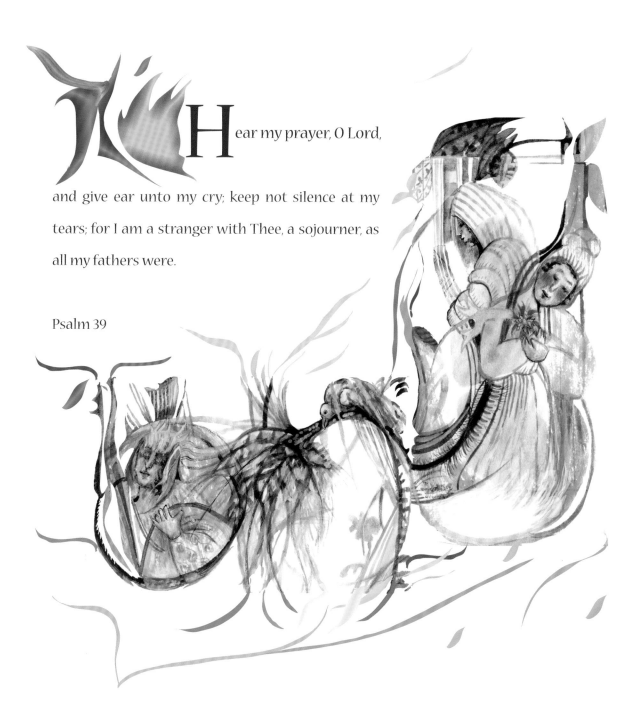

Hear my prayer, O Lord,
and give ear unto my cry; keep not silence at my
tears; for I am a stranger with Thee, a sojourner, as
all my fathers were.

Psalm 39

Rabbi Levi Yithzak was a Hasidic master whose dearest child, his only son, died. The funeral bier was taken through the village and the congregation followed behind in deep silence.

Of course the Rabbi himself was walking behind his son's bier. And then to the great astonishment of his people, he began to dance. He began a slow, grave dance with his coattails flying out like great black wings.

The people began to look at each other and they at last had to say something, and they said," What are you doing? What are you doing!"

And he said to them, "A pure soul was rendered to me, and a pure soul I render back"…and he danced, even with heartbreak and death.

Susan Murphy, *Upside Down Zen*

Do not rely on your own understanding.

Proverbs 3:5

All love that depends on physical cause will pass away once the cause is no longer there. But that love which is not dependent on a physical cause will never pass away.

Avot 5:19

Yου have counted my wanderings,

placed my tears in your flask,

are they not in your record?

Psalm 56:9

Midrash

Rabbi Shimon Ben Pazzi said of this verse, in the name of R. Jehoshua Ben Levi who in turn spoke in the name of Bar Kappara:

When a person sheds tears over the death or pain of another, the Holy Blessed One counts each and every tear and stores them in his/her private treasury flask. Indeed! The Presence preserves these tears because they will become the *"tal,"* fresh dew, which will be used to revive the dead at the end of time.

Attributed to Mahari Pinto

by Rabbi Avrohom Chaim Feuer, *Tehilim Treasury*

Love is strong as death,
jealousy is cruel as the grave
(Song of Songs)

because at the hour of a man's death the parting of the soul from the body is difficult, for there is no love and no attachment and no mixture like that of the soul and the body; and jealousy is cruel as the grave, because there is no jealousy in the world like that of the man who goes to his grave and sees that the world still lives.

Commentary by Elijah ben Shlomo Zalman, the Gaon of Vilna, Lithuania, (1720–1797)

 **I** may not be able to perceive it right now,

but The Holy One fills all creation, being is made of God, you and I,

everything is made of God - even the grains of sand beneath my feet,

the whole world is included and therefore utterly nullified within

God - while I, in my stubborn insistence on my own autonomy and

independence, only succeed in banishing myself from any possibility

of meaning whatsoever.

R. Kalonymous Kalman Shapira of Piaseszne (1889–1943)

Benei Makshava Tova, found buried in the Warsaw Ghetto 1943.

While a messenger was yet speaking, there came also another, and said: "Your sons and daughters were eating and drinking wine in their eldest brother's house; and behold, there came a great wind from across the wilderness and smote the four corners of the house, and it fell upon the young people, and they are dead. Only I, by myself, escaped to tell you."

Then Job arose and rent his mantle, and
shaved his head and fell down upon the
ground and worshipped; and he said:

Naked came I out of my mother's womb,
And naked shall I return thither;
The Lord gave,
and the Lord hath taken away;
Blessed be the name of the Lord.

Job 1:18-21

87

The *Kaddish* is our way of consoling the Divine Mourner and expressing sympathy for The Great Name.

The Divine Royal One cherishes the life of each and every being and considers the death of even a single one a defeat that diminishes His/Her greatness and desecrates Her/His Holy Name. Thus when a human being dies, The Great Name has lost a reality and thereby suffers diminution. We console God, as it were, by praying for the restoration of Her/His Greatness.

An interpretation of the writings of
Rav Simchah Bunam of P'shischa, Poland (1787–1859)
and Israeli Nobel laureate Shmuel Yosaf Agnon (1888–1970)

Consider the work of God;

for who can make that straight, which He hath made crooked? In the day of prosperity be joyful, and in the day of adversity consider: God hath made even the one as well as the other, to the end that man should find nothing after him.

Ecclesiastes 7:13

R abbi Meir

lost both his sons one Sabbath afternoon while he studied at the House of Learning. When he returned and asked for his sons, his wife, Beruryah, evaded his question and asked him to chant the blessing for the departing Sabbath. Then, she gave him dinner. He ate while his anxiety for his sons grew. After the meal, he asked about the boys and Beruryah answered with a question. "If a friend gives us something to hold for safekeeping, aren't we obligated to return it without complaint whenever she asks?"

The rabbi, surprised that his wife would ask something he was sure she knew, said, "Of course. You know you must return what has been deposited with you." Gently, she led him to the room where both boys lay dead. She removed the cover from their faces. Rabbi Meir cried out in grief. His wife spoke gently, reminding him about their obligation to return what is not theirs, no matter the preciousness, without complaint. Beruryah uttered the words of Job (1:21), "The Lord gave and the Lord taketh away: blessed be the Name of the Lord."

story from the Talmud, Midrash Proverbs 31

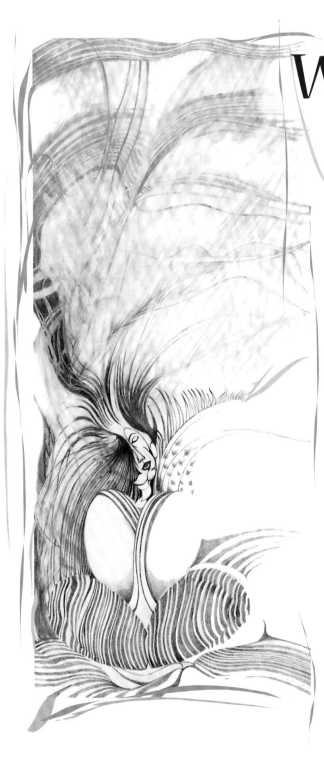

When Creation returned
and tapped my shoulder
I fell into a dream,

my course as set
as the birds in the sky
and the seasons of whales
who, laughing in air and water, sing.
What grace!

We are captives
as the stream in its banks
as the season of tears or toil moves to joy.

We who leave in sorrow, carrying our seeds,
will return happy with the harvest.
We come home,
rejoice in our bindings and green.

Psalm 126   A Song of Ascent

An Interpretation by Hyla Shifra Bolsta

Our life

is mist, a breath, a wisp of smoke, our days on earth transient as a shadow.

Job 8:9

PART IV

NOTES

GLOSSARY

ACKNOWLEDGMENTS

A Note on God

In the paintings and text throughout this book, God, He, She and It, are interchanged with The Great Name. The term "God" acts as a symbol, an open evocation of a vast metaphysical reality.

All characteristics and descriptions are figurative.

Commonly, English language prayer books (especially non-contemporary), refer to a masculine God. This is a convention and convenience. Hebrew words are either masculine or feminine. For example, Jews consider The Shechinah (a feminine noun), a feminine manifestation of God.

The variations are used without bias.

NAMES OF GOD USED IN THIS BOOK

Creation

HaShem

Ein Sof

Master of the
Universe

Shechina

The Bird Shechina

The Blessed

The Creator

The Divine Name

The Divine Mourner

The Divine Royal One

The Great Compassion

The Great Name

The Great Teacher

The Holy Blessed One

The Holy One

The Infinite Light

The Majestic One

The Name

The Nameless One

The Presence

The Ruler

The Queen

This Infinite Understanding

A ladder stood on the earth, and the top of it reached to heaven (Genesis 28:12) This is prayer.

Zohar

Prayer and its essence are the foundation of the Torah. With prayer, we come to recognize and appreciate the greatness of God. And when we pray with calm, open minds and hearts, we awaken the "rational" soul to love of God.

A Teaching of R. Shneur Zalman of Liadi, (1745–1812), the founder of Chabad.

He wrote *Lessons in Tanya*, a fundamental text of Chabad Chassidic philosophy. *Tanya* is the initial word of the book, which is also called *Likkutei Amarim* (*Collected Discourses*) and *Sefer shel Beinonim* (*The Book of the Intermediates*).

NOTES ON AMEN

Amen is an abbreviation of "*Ayl Melech Nehehman*" (God is a faithful King). One religious teaching explains that when a person says Amen total faith in God should be expressed, which gives rise to a feeling of peace and serenity in Paradise. Likewise, repeating Amen by rote or routine, half-heartedly or incompletely, shows ignorance and a lack of respect for its power. In fact, some have taught that it is better to remain silent than to say Amen without appreciation of its great power.

Another teaching tell us that when the congregation utters Amen it is as if every member has recited the blessing and identified with it as the Truth.

Traditionally, the power and importance of this word was considered so great that for those who proclaimed it with strong spirit and sincere devotion, the gates of Paradise were opened.

Throughout the *Tanach* (the Five Books of Moses, Prophets and Writings), Amen is used for emphatic agreement with a blessing (or curse). "So be it!" "May *Ha Shem* do so!" or "Truly!" "And let us respond (or say) Amen is found in the Prophets, Numbers, Psalms, Deuteronomy and Jeremiah. The *Kaddish* is almost completely written in Aramaic, yet this phrase is written in Hebrew, harkening back to these various Biblical texts.

The sages categorized three branches of thought within this phrase: agreement with the ideas set forth in the prayer, acceptance of the Will of God and faith in God.

In a text by Maimonides (1135–1204), Amen indicated the end of a phrase.

In his treatise *Sefer HaRokeach*, (*The Compounder of Spices*), Eleazar ben Judah of Worms (c. 1160–1238), explained that Rav Joshua ben Gadya declared: "One who says Amen in this world is granted the privilege of responding Amen in the World to Come."

Notes of interest, summarized from *The Kaddish: Its History and Significance*, by David Telsner, Tal Orot Institute, Jerusalem, 1995

Every prayer in the *siddur* is taken from the Bible, either word for word or paraphrased from a Biblical verse. The same is true for the *Kaddish*.

Its opening phrase comes from Ezekiel 38:23. He introduces the End of Days and the Messianic era, and prophesies a time when all nations of the world will know the sanctity and greatness of *HaShem*. God speaks through Ezekiel and proclaims, "I will be exalted and sanctified." Thus will *HaShem* redeem the people of the earth. The last two phrases were added later. The first, a prayer for peace and life refers to the great desire of The Creator and all Creation for peace, giving voice to passages in Isaiah and Psalms.

      The last phrase comes from Job - that the Almighty in heaven will grant peace on earth - and Isaiah, who had full belief that the Lord will establish peace for us. Scholars have discussed the last line over the centuries, and given various interpretations of its significance.

      Ideas include the eternal life of angels and the end of death (Rav Obadiah Sforno, 1475-1550), the harmony of nature even though it contains opposing forces (Malbim, Bible commentator, 19th century) and the idea that this passage is a statement that peace resides in the heavens where *HaShem* rules and therefore it originates there as well (Amos Hakham, 20th century).

The *Kaddish* is set in language that implies both the imperative and the future. Some say this alludes to the idea that Judaism carries a forward looking view of human affairs since The Messiah and Redemption are yet to come and not dominated by physical limitations or political interests. Rather, the Jewish outlook is about spiritual well being.

According to Rabbi Nosson Scherman, "the effect of *Kaddish* was well known in the time of the Talmud" (200 C.E.–500 C.E.).

And the earliest text that connects an orphaned child's prayers to the soul of a deceased parent is the interpretive work, *Tanna D'bei Eliyahu* (circa 400).

In medieval times the rabbis and community used earlier teachings as the basis for the universal custom to recite *Kaddish* as a source of merit for the departed soul.

The *Kaddish* text appears first in the prayer book, *Siddur* (circa 860).

The first recorded mention of an orphan reciting the *Kaddish* as a custom is found in *Sefer HaRokeach* of Rabbi Elazar of Germany (circa 1200).

The first mention of mourners reciting *Kaddish* at the end of the service is in *Or Zarua*, by Rabbi Yitzhak ben Moshe of Vienna (circa 1400).

Rabbi Moses Isserles of Cracow, Poland, mentions the custom of reciting the prayer for eleven months after a parent dies (circa 1550).

During the Middle Ages in Germany, it became a prayer for mourners and was called *Kaddish Yatom*, Orphan's Prayer, especially for minors, said at the end of services.

In contemporary times, some congregations say *Kaddish* in unison, in solidarity with the mourners. In others, it is customary for the mourners to stand and recite *Kaddish* together, while the remainder of the congregation responds at different points.

Notes on when Kaddish is recited

Sitting Shiva

After the burial (unless it falls directly before or on *Shabbat*), the mourners sit *shiva* in the home of one of the mourners. *Shiva* is Hebrew for seven and this period of total immersion of attention on the deceased loved one lasts for seven days. Each day a *minyan* is gathered in the home and a service is conducted that includes the recitation of the *Kaddish*.

Yahrzeit

Yahrzeit, a Yiddish word, means "a year's time." It is the anniversary of the death of a parent or loved one and is commemorated generally on the date of death, following the Hebrew calendar. Traditionally, a *yahrzeit* candle is lit at sunset the evening before the date, burns for twenty-four hours and is allowed to extinguish itself. The mourner attends synagogue services and recites *Kaddish* at least once on this day.

Yizkor Services

Yizkor, a Hebrew word, means remember. It is Judaism's memorial service. The *Yizkor* prayers are recited in the synagogue during four holidays, on the last day of the Festivals of *Pesach*, *Shavuot*, *Sukkot* and on *Yom Kippur*, toward the end of the day. The *Kaddish* is included in these services. Those who recite the prayers are those who have lost one or both of their parents.

There are various ways to remember the anniversary dates, such as a *Yahrzeit* Diary, with the Name, Hebrew name, Date and Hebrew date listed. Also listed is the grave location record which has the name, cemetery, location and route directions and the section, block and grave number.

Chabad - a philosophical (spiritual/religous) movement founded by R. Schneur Zalman of Liadi. It is an acronym for three Hebrew words: *Chochmah* (Wisdom, Creative power, Insight), *Binah* (Intuition, Understanding, Intelligence,) and *Da-at* (Knowledge: higher, hidden, lower and extended).

daven - Yiddish word for "to recite prayers," specifically in the Jewish style where each word is spoken quietly or aloud in chant, used by Jews of European origin.

derash - creative interpretation, exposition, sermon

devukut - cleaving; in kabbalistic literature, communion with God, described as the highest step on the spiritual ladder

doxology - prayer of praise

Gaon - medieval Jewish scholar, honorable sage, Torah genius - to be considered a gaon is one of the highest forms of praise

HaShem - name for God, literally The Name, both and neither masculine or feminine or plural

Kabbalah - mystical school of thought based on the Torah and Jewish religious law. Its aim is to understand God and describe concepts that are basically indescribable, for example, infinity. To that end, it describes God as *Ein Sof*, which in Hebrew means "without end" and *Bal Tachlis*, which in Hebrew means "He is not bound in any way." There are numerous ways in which the text describes the many aspects God, including both masculine and feminine qualities.

kavanah - intention, conscious thought, concentration

midrash - commentary on texts using metaphor, stories, imagery, associative ideas and various literary devices that bring added meaning to texts. The Midrash is also a collection of many works of homilies and creative interpretations written by Talmudic sages and is one of the accompaniments to the Tanach.

minyan - quorum of ten people required in order to hold a prayer service in community, at the synagogue. Traditionally, it was ten men, currently many congregations include women. A *minyan* is needed to say *Kaddish*.

Rav; **Reb** - Rabbi

sephirot - emanations, in Jewish mysticism, the emanations from the essence of God that interact with the universe

Shabbat - Sabbath, day of rest

Shechina - the Divine Presence, often in the feminine aspect

shiva - seven. The mourners "sit *shiva*" for seven days. It is a time when all attention of mourners is devoted to the newly deceased loved one. A *minyan* gathers in the home of the mourners and a service is held each day that includes the recitation of the *Kaddish*.

siddur - Jewish prayer book used on *Shabbat* and weekdays throughout the year

supernal - celestial, heavenly, coming from the heavens or a higher place

tal - dew

Talmud - repository of oral law (Mishnah and Gemara)

Tanach - the Five Books of Moses, Prophets and Writings

Yahrzeit - the anniversary date of the death of a parent or loved one, generally based on the Hebrew calendar

Yizkor - service - memorial service

Zohar - Hebrew, translated as *The Splendor* or *The Brilliiance*, it is the primary written work in the mystical tradition of the Kabbalah

Acknowledgments

Thank you to my publisher, Bernie Scharfstein. His generosity, sense of humor, fairness and excellent suggestions have made working with him not only a true partnership, but one filled with enjoyment and satisfaction.

Thank you to those who endorsed the manuscript so that I could find a publisher.

Rabbi Margaret Holub envisioned my paintings as part of a book that would contribute to the worldwide community of Jews. She encouraged me to engage in a project I previously thought was the realm of Rabbis and Talmudic Scholars. We analyzed each word and phrase together. Her enthusiasm and insights during our study sessions were an inspiration. And Margaret suggested that I contact her former teacher, Rabbi Lewis Barth, PhD. He carefully reviewed my commentaries, corrected the illuminated calligraphic Aramaic/Hebrew text, and gave approval to the project. Rabbi Avram Davis, PhD., added to my joy as he nurtured me with unconditional support and fostered this project from the beginning. Rabbi DovBer Pinson, Dr. Jonathan Boyarin and Rabbi Lawrence Kushner supported the project based on reviewed samples.

Thank you to those who gave input at the inception of the project and to those whose faith in me and the project sustained and nourished it over the six years of work.

Fran Schwartz represented the *Kaddish* Series to Jewish museums. Kate Gale, PhD., Red Hen Press, connected me to authors, including Marc Kaminsky, who referred me to author Allan Appel who suggested others for review and feedback. Charlotte Cook, Charlotte Gullick, Irene Thomas, PhD., and Lillian Reiter edited texts. Joel Schwartz offered his expertise in finding grants.

Janis Krug's artistic eyes and perceptions made for improvements, as did Cliff Glover and Marion Miller, who gave me their critical, aesthetic sensibilities so that significant changes were made during the first few years. Meg Courtney's practical insights eliminated important flaws.

Linda Jupiter's thoughtfulness, patience, scrutiny of detail, last minute suggestions, high standards and adeptness in book production, plus help with computer problems, have been notable and significant gifts.

A special thanks to Len Lyons, author of six books including *The Ethiopian Jews of Israel*, who became my mentor. He gave many hours of his time, insights into publishing, enthusiasm for this manuscript, experience and assistance in networking so that this book would find its way into print.

Thank you to friends and those I have not met who helped in numerous ways over the years. I thank all for their advice, feedback, suggestions, networking help and earnest care.

Sonke Adlung, Kathleen Barbero, Donald Bartlett, Annie Beckett, Bernie Beckman, David Biale, Bob Blumenthal, Dimitri Budker, Lorna Catford, Michelle Cherrin, Christie Olsen Day, Helene Dunbar, Michael Ezra, Patrick Goley, Kathy Guest, Polly Green, Jerry Greenberg, Ocean Alexis Halbert, Matthew Harris, Mettika Hoffman, Hannie Van Horen, Rosamund Jorgensen, Altie Karper, Tony Kemp, Mirka Knaster, Michael Larsen, Jill Lopate, Catherine Madsen, Elizabeth Pomada, Bruce Robinson, Naomi Schneider, Michael Sittenfield, Frances Spiegel, Maggie Watson.

Thank you to anyone I inadvertently overlooked and to those who have purchased prints of the paintings that are part of this book.

Thank you to my son, Aharon, for his care, considerations, pivotal comments and unfaltering insistence that I give proper dimension to my art by keeping a large format for this book.

Thank you to my husband, Jack, whose steadfast support, tireless encouragement, crucial aesthetic and practical suggestions, belief in my artistry and creativity, helped me create this work. He suggested key ideas that are part of the foundation of this manuscript. His loving kindness gave me the nourishment to sustain continued work on this project for more than six years. His patience for my dogged insistence on perfection and the frustrations that came with it, are not taken for granted, as well as help with mathematical proportions and other vexations. His cooking, serving and all the other little things that supported me to finish, no matter the pitfalls, are part of his enduring, special character.

Lastly, I am thankful for the grace bestowed on me throughout the project. May this work be a life-affirming contribution to its readers.

ABOUT THE AUTHOR/ILLUSTRATOR

Hyla Shifra Bolsta has drawn and painted since early childhood. As a young teen she studied life drawing at The Art Student's League in New York City. She is a graduate of Pratt Institute, New York City, and recipient of a two-year fellowship grant from the Fine Arts Work Center (FAWC), Provincetown, Massachusetts. She also earned a Master's Degree in psychology at Sonoma State University, California. Her professional work includes book and book cover illustration, layout and design. She is represented in collections throughout the USA, Europe and Israel.

Hyla lives with her husband Jack on the northern California coast, where she creates art in various media, writes, reads and gardens, and enjoys the spectacular environment with bike rides through forests and walks on beaches and headlands. Their son is a professional musician situated in the San Francisco bay area.

Hyla engages in Jewish study with Rabbi Margaret Holub as a member of the Mendocino Coast Jewish Community. She also is a student of Rabbi Avram Davis, studying Chasidism. On occasion, she gives teachings that are accompanied by her unique and entertaining pictures.

ABOUT THE TYPE AND ART

Two typefaces are used in this book, Nueva Std (brown) and Papyrus (blue, in Part II).

Part I, the illuminated calligraphic texts, are pen and ink and brushed black and white gouache.
Part II, the paintings, are gouache.
Both are on Arches watercolor block paper, either cold or hot pressed.

Throughout the book there are sections of scanned images from earlier work, executed in a variety of media: oils, acrylics, charcoal, pencil and pen and ink drawings. These images have been manipulated in Photoshop and InDesign and freely cut and cropped.

All embellishments are computer generated with a drawing tablet or mouse. By utilizing computer techniques in conjunction with traditional media used for illuminated manuscripts, I consider that I have created a truly contemporary illuminated manuscript.